Tales of Twilight: Verses of Mythical Creatures and Fairytales

Alethea B.H. Harper

BookLeaf Publishing

India | USA | UK

Presentation by *BookLeaf Publishing*

Web: www.bookleafpub.com

E-mail: info@bookleafpub.com

ISBN: 9789360946791

First edition 2024

For my mom,

her constant love and

support gave me the

courage to follow my dreams.

ACKNOWLEDGEMENT

I want to thank my family, friends, therapist, Katrina Howard, and everyone in my support network. Most of all, I thank God for all my blessings. This book would not be possible without my Lord and Savior or the people who surround me.

PREFACE

Welcome to this collection of poems about the myths, legends, and fairytales that have captured our imaginations for generations. These stories have stood the test of time, inspiring countless retellings and adaptations. They have comforted and challenged us and continue to hold a place in our hearts and minds.

This book contains a series of poems that explore these tales in new and exciting ways. Each poem is a unique interpretation of a familiar story, offering fresh insights and perspectives on characters and events we thought we knew so well. Some poems make you smile, others make you think, and others tug at your heartstrings.

As you read through this collection, I hope you will experience the same joy and fascination I felt while writing these poems. These timeless stories can enrich our lives and help us understand ourselves and the world in new ways.

So take a deep breath, turn the page, and be transported to a world of myths, legends, and fairy tales. Enjoy the journey.

October 1989 (Inspired by I Go Back to May 1937 By Sharon Olds)

I gaze at my mother, replenishing her thirst at
the water fountain as my father silently
approaches her.
She turns, his masculine presence startling her.

A princess surrounded by light and

a prince born from darkness.

This is the beginning: simple, sweet, beautiful.
The sight before me turns sullen as I know their
future.
Marriage of two becomes a family of four.
Simple becomes complicated.
Sweet becomes sour.
Beautiful becomes ugly.

He will bestow pain and hurt;
Upon his wife and children.
This knowledge would shock the young woman
before me.
Who gazes at the man with sparkles in her eyes.
I should stop this to save my mother from him.
Before he becomes unrecognizable, a shell that
lets his fears destroy his love. In truth, the
fairytale that started at Cinderella Knitting Mill
is a must-have. Without it, I would not have my
life, family, or memories.
I cherish them even if the ending resembles the
Grimm fairy tales.

Nyami Nyami

River
God, Zambezi is
A snake, fish, dragon, or
Whirlpool; he stains the water red as
He swims.

Iele (Inspired Her Kind by Anne Sexton)

I dream of soaring among the stars.
Only to wake in the darkest hour of the night.
I relish the sensation of freedom, a life with no bars.
I dash to the forest illuminated by moonlight.
An air of playfulness swirls around me like a wheel.
Giving me joy that burns bright.
I am an Iele.

I dream of my kin and me living in the sky,
Only touching the ground to dance by the fire.
Our steps are fun and spry.

Creating moments in life in which we never tire.
Whether we are solid or immaterial, we are
surreal
With our dainty feet sinking into the grass and
mire.
I am an Iele.

I dream of men whose last gaze is upon our
show—
Seduced by our wild hair and siren song of bells.
We are immortals that fill hearts with woe.
Our tempers are hidden behind our beauty that
quells.
A circle of mushrooms is all that is left of the
ordeal,
Along with stories of loved ones gone with no
farewells.
I am an Iele.

Petrified Beauty

Female. Maiden. Woman. I was once this.
In a world that is now crumbled to dust,
When creatures and Gods roamed in the mist,
Being young and beautiful was a must,
Though dangerous, for it stirred men's lust.
For which women were punished threefold.
It happened to me, trapped in a man's hold.
Raided by the sea and cursed by the owl.
I'm a villain whose gaze will turn you cold.
If you find me, I will end you with a scowl.

Nessie's Vexed

Loch Ness is the name, but call me Ness.
The humans wait for me to egress.
With their boats and trawls;
I tire of their drawls.
So, I appear, and they bolt. Success!

A Golden Feast, A Silver Treat

Alicanto, birds of night
Have wings that shine bright.
Men follow its path in search of plunder;
Only to watch as the riches are devoured by its
hunger.

Small Pearl

Hidden among the household, like
Sand on a beach.

She's a slave with a quiet soul
and a clever mind.

Her worth is only seen through
what she offers

To the men who
leave her behind. Forty thieves came for her
master's
life for knowing their secret.

She fouled their plans
and none survived.

This made her a gem in Ali Baba's eyes;
so he made her his son's wife.

They did not realize she was
born a pure pearl that thrived.

Mami Wata

Mother
Of water with
A mirror in her hand.
Her presence is a gift for those
She takes.

Just Dance

Red shoes are beautiful,
Expensive and sophisticated, and I loved mine.
Dancing without any control over my
Steps were my curse for idolizing shoes.
Having them did not make me happy in the end.
Once I prayed to God, I received help. I was
Easily filled with happiness, and my
Soul found rest in Heaven.

Isis Unveil

A Goddess to the land where
the world began.

A wife, healer,
mourner and mother.

At first, she was obscure
but she lived up to her name.

Her place as a deity stands
on aiding those who suffer.

Mirror's Whispering Secrets

Everyone talks about the Princess
and the Queen.

I am the real victim,
trapped in this reflector.

Staring at the world
that I can never experience.

Seen only as a dusty
relic in the castle's forgotten sector.

Leprechauns Fortune

Fairies or goblins?
Our species is null. Call us
Guardians of Gold.

Crimson Roots

Death can breed new life.
For a dragon died, and
its blood spilled from its body.
The Earth drank every drop.
From that sacrifice bore a Blood Tree.
A giver of medicines and dyes.
Paying it forward to the temporal beings.

The Villainous Enchantress

Morgan le Fay,
Once a princess married away.
A powerful enchantress and a mother.
She hadn't an occasion to plot against her
brother!

An Unkindness

We are drawn to the children of battle
that have entered into eternal rest.

We take their life's essence to Odin's Hall.
Our onus is to serve the fighters' mead.

We are lovers of mortals and heroes.
Royal women who appear with ravens.

Ode to my Sister, the Seamstress

A princess with six brothers, all
Hidden by their father in a castle
From his new bride
That threatened their very existence,

However, the witch was observant.
To her husband's schemes and found the
Twine he used as a guide
To his lineage, where she hexed six,

Of his offspring, but the girl was overlooked
She escaped the Queen's wrath, and she ran
To a cabin to hide
But her brothers follow her in their bird forms,

Waiting for night, they became human once
again
Revealing to their sibling how to alter their fate
With sweaters, she must provide
While she lives in stillness as she creates their
star,

Flower garments using asters while shrouded,
In loneliness, six years was the goal, but in year
four, when
A King with pride
Found her and intertwined their lives together,

Even though she could not speak or laugh, she
continued to sew
The Queen's mother found her unfit, so when
her new daughter
Gave birth, she lied
About why the babies were no longer alive,

Which enraged her husband, so he
Chose to burn her and to a stake,
she was tied
But her brothers arrived in the nick of time,
Stalling the executioner while their sister threw
them
Their freedom from the spell while flames licked
at her body

Her brothers, without breaking their stride
Turned from birds to men saving their sister
from the fiery inferno,

And now free from the curse, the savior finally
speaks,
Spilling all of her pain, sadness, and loss caused
by
The deceitful Queen Mother
Which revealed the snake among them and

The mother of the King tried to save herself
By divulging the children were safe, but her son
was clear-eyed
He destroyed his mother and reunited his family,
Their happiness is only because of the princess
Whose heart had been obliterated by the sorrow
Her strength could not be denied
For she is the reason the story ends with a
happily ever after.

The Rare Hunt

White as a dove,
the enchanted unicorn
roamed the land, symbolizing peace
and innocence within the realms of mortals.

Where there is light,
Darkness will emerge. It came in the form of
selfish men with
eyes that declared the corruption in their souls.

The hunters drove
into the forest to procure the beautiful horn.
For, it made any sickness cease.
They were creatures that were pursued until
there were no more mare immortals.

The Origin Story of the Queen of Flowers

Before becoming
A flower in the earth, I
was a beautiful
Nymph that took her last breath, with
Only the weeds and soil for comfort.

Persephone's Plight

A flower trapped in a cage.
A goddess of life and renewal
surrounded by souls who have reached the end.

Her mother's rage
made the world cold and cruel
Until her daughter could ascend.

She can only engage
with the world for a short time to refuel.
Winter is when nature dies, and she must
descend.

Persephone, a wife and mother, is stuck
in a constant nightmare.
That turns her only daughter into the bringer of
such horror.

Eternal Springs

The fountain of youth
gives people a second chance.

The irony is that many
die before the water can grace their lips.

Tool of War

Handsome, I am not.
I'm equal parts scorpion and man.
My path was forged to spill blood in battle.
However, my passion is to save those in danger.

The Shimmering Guardian

I emerge from the blue flames.
The protector of the western skies
I walk the dirt paths as a human invisible among
the villagers.
I roam the jungle, my white and striped fur
stained brown by the earth.

As a human, I am shunned.
As an animal, I am hunted and maimed.
I'm forced into a cage made of wood for wealth
and distraction.
Humans unknowingly doomed themselves to a
world without morality and justice.

The Isle of the Sea Turtle

Captivating. Lush. Green.
The island is in the middle of the sea.
It offers salvation to ocean voyagers.
Setting foot upon the soft grass, sailors seek to quench
their thirst and quiet the raging hunger within
their bellies.

Fire. Pain. Anger.
Alas, the moment of serenity ends;
As the land beneath their feet shifts.
The men cower as they rise toward the skies
Only to plummet into the dark depths of
Neptune's abode.

Dark. Cold. Alone.
Souls taken by the watery expanse;
For the island was a child of the sea.
A turtle that carries a home on its back for
others;
Constantly searching for a refuge that it will
never find.

The Scream of Death

She's alone among the mounds,
Eyes like red berries found on the mountain ash.
Haunting and fair, a maiden that forever weeps.
When you hear her scream, the end is near.
She is Death's Harbinger.